People in My Community

Police Officer

by Jacqueline Laks Gorman
Photographs by Gregg Andersen

Reading consultant: Susan Nations, M.Ed., author/literacy coach/consultant

WEEKLY WR READER®
EARLY LEARNING LIBRARY

Please visit our web site at: **www.earlyliteracy.cc**
For a free color catalog describing Weekly Reader® Early Learning Library's
list of high-quality books, call 1-877-445-5824 (USA) or 1-800-387-3178 (Canada).
Weekly Reader® Early Learning Library's fax: (414) 336-0164.

Library of Congress Cataloging-in-Publication Data

Gorman, Jacqueline Laks, 1955-
    Police officer / by Jacqueline Laks Gorman.
      p. cm. — (People in my community)
    Summary: Explains what police officers do, including helping people
in trouble, stopping people who break the law, and directing traffic.
    Includes bibliographical references and index.
    ISBN 0-8368-3297-3 (lib. bdg.)
    ISBN 0-8368-3304-X (softcover)
    1. Police—Juvenile literature. [1. Police. 2. Occupations.] I. Title.
HV7922.G67   2002
363.2'2—dc21
                        2002024622

This edition first published in 2002 by
Weekly Reader® Early Learning Library
330 West Olive Street, Suite 100
Milwaukee, WI 53212 USA

Art direction and page layout: Tammy Gruenewald
Photographer: Gregg Andersen
Editorial assistant: Diane Laska-Swanke
Production: Susan Ashley

Printed in the United States of America

1 2 3 4 5 6 7 8 9 06 05 04 03 02

Note to Educators and Parents

Reading is such an exciting adventure for young children! They are beginning to integrate their oral language skills with written language. To encourage children along the path to early literacy, books must be colorful, engaging, and interesting; they should invite the young reader to explore both the print and the pictures.

People in My Community is a new series designed to help children read about the world around them. In each book young readers will learn interesting facts about some familiar community helpers.

Each book is specially designed to support the young reader in the reading process. The familiar topics are appealing to young children and invite them to read — and re-read — again and again. The full-color photographs and enhanced text further support the student during the reading process.

In addition to serving as wonderful picture books in schools, libraries, homes, and other places where children learn to love reading, these books are specifically intended to be read within an instructional guided reading group. This small group setting allows beginning readers to work with a fluent adult model as they make meaning from the text. After children develop fluency with the text and content, the book can be read independently. Children and adults alike will find these books supportive, engaging, and fun!

— Susan Nations, M.Ed., author, literacy coach, and consultant in literacy development

The police officer has an important job. The police officer helps people.

The police officer helps people in trouble. The police officer helps people in danger.

Police officers wear badges and special clothes. They use **radios** to talk to each other.

radio

Police officers stop people who break the law. Sometimes they use **handcuffs**.

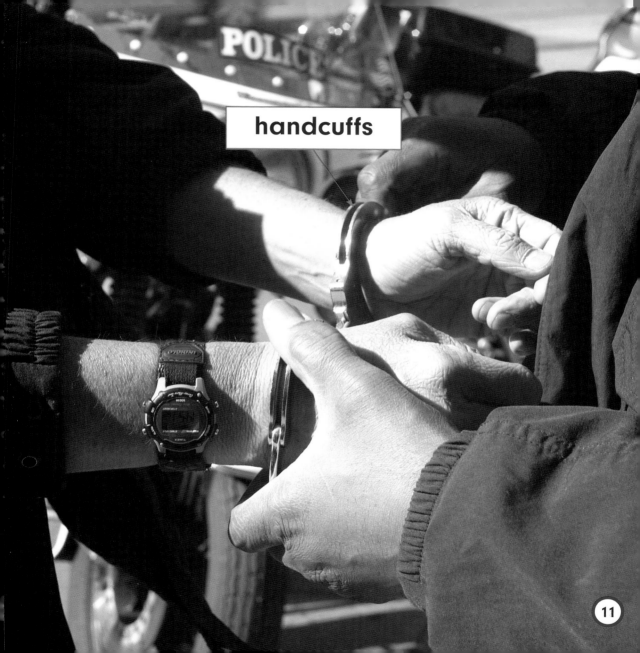

handcuffs

11

Sometimes police officers ride in police cars or on **motorcycles**. Sometimes they ride on horseback.

motorcycles

Sometimes police officers direct traffic. They give tickets to drivers who drive too fast.

Sometimes police officers visit schools. They talk to you about keeping safe.

If you are ever lost or need help, you should talk to a police officer.

It looks like fun to be a police officer. Would you like to be a police officer some day?

Glossary

badges — small signs that identify people and that are pinned to their clothes

danger — something that is not safe

handcuffs — metal rings that are locked around someone's wrists

law — a rule that people follow for the good of everyone

For More Information

Fiction Books

Rathmann, Peggy. *Officer Buckle and Gloria.* New York: Putnam, 1995.

Yee, Wong Herbert. *The Officer's Ball.* Boston: Houghton Mifflin, 1997.

Nonfiction Books

Greene, Carol. *Police Officers Protect People.* Plymouth, Minn.: Child's World, 1997.

Kottke, Jan. *A Day with Police Officers.* New York: Children's Press, 2000.

Schaefer, Lola M. *We Need Police Officers.* Mankato, Minn.: Pebble Books, 2000.

Web Sites

Police Are My Friends Coloring Book
www.hendersonville-pd.org/kids/coloringbook
A picture book about police officers to print out, read, and color

Index

About the Author

Jacqueline Laks Gorman is a writer and editor. She grew up in New York City and began her career working on encyclopedias and other reference books. Since then, she has worked on many different kinds of books. She lives with her husband and children, Colin and Caitlin, in DeKalb, Illinois.